The Good Stuff

Quips and Tips on Life, Love, Work and Happiness

by America's Top Humorista
Christine Holton Cashen, MAEd, CSP

D1016835

For bulk purchases, call 1.800.706.0152

Published by DC Murphy Publishing, Dallas, Texas

Cover photos by Anne Silverman, www.AnneSilvermanPhotography.com
Edited by Debbie Johnson, Spike Communications, www.SpikeCommunications.com
Book Design by Formation Studio, www.FormationStudio.com
Illustrations by Tami Evans, www.TamiEvans.com

Printed in the USA

ISBN: 978-1-61658-980-6

Dedicated to the BEST STUFF in my life –

Husband Gregg, calm amidst chaos

Wondrous children, Donovan and Camille

Amazing parents, who always pushed me to go for it
(without you I wouldn't be here... seriously!)

Cool Reader,

This is the spot where I'm supposed to explain exactly when that amazing light bulb moment occurred that inspired this book. Easy answer. It wasn't even my idea!

As a speaker, one of the most enjoyable parts of making presentations is the opportunity to chat with participants following my talks. Without fail people would say, *"I wish my _____ (fill in the blank: husband, boss, friend, co-worker) was in attendance to hear your program. Do you have a book that I could take home?"* So after much prodding and perfect storm connecting, I've finally put together some of my favorite creative and practical ideas to make life better.

Fast forward. So at long last I could respond, *"Yes... I'm writing a book!"* Then of course the obligatory follow-up question: *"What's the title?"* I was embarrassed to say that I didn't know. All I could say was that is was *"really good stuff."* And so the title was born.

My hope is that a read through (or even a quick browse or skim) will provide you with easy-to-implement ideas that will truly make your personal and professional life better and happier.

Now listen: we are all busy and picking up a huge text on happiness sounds good, but who has time for such a heavy read these days? **The Good Stuff** is the perfect quick read – with a huge impact. Big ideas laid out in an easy-to-digest format. Perfect, right?!

So, please continue on hip reader, and enjoy the good stuff....

Christine

PS... And of course, if you have "good stuff" to share, I'd love your feedback at www.ChristineCashen.com

The Good Stuff
Table of Contents

The Good Stuff

1

People Bug Me

Rules Rules Rules

Don't you hate it when people don't know the rules? We all have rules for other people that they don't even know about – but they should! I'm okay and you're not! Isn't that what most people think? I try to have a good sense of humor, but it's hard because people bug me! It's amazing what some people consider *"rules"* while others simply have no idea they are breaking them. If the world just knew the *"rules"* for appropriate behavior, there would be far less stress, less conflict, and we'd all have happier and healthier relationships.

At almost every presentation I give, I do an informal poll asking what bugs people the most. Some of the top offenders include inappropriate cell phone use, road rage issues and non-pooper-scoopers.

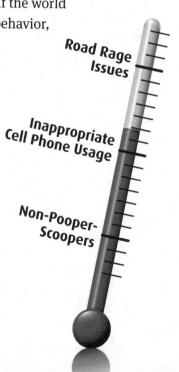

Humorista's Top 10 Socially Obvious Rules
(that aren't so obvious)

10 Always use your turn signal

9 If you aren't driving faster than me in the left lane, move over PRONTO!

8 If something in the fridge is empty, toss it!

7 Don't be a loud cell phone talker

6 Put your shopping cart back in the corral

5 Let people off the elevator before you get on

4 If I let you in while driving, give me the thank you wave

3 If you're within a 20 foot radius of my desk, don't e-mail me... walk over!

2 Don't be a grocery store express-lane violator

1 TP always over the top

TP Issues – Your Way or Mine?

There are so many home vexations. Wouldn't home life be more tranquil if everyone put empty containers away, stopped slurping coffee and PUT THE SEAT DOWN! In fact, when I mention that toilet paper goes over the top, many people go wild in agreement. Of course there are always those bewildered few who look around like everyone else is crazy. They really don't care which way the paper goes on the roll. They're just happy that

someone replaced the cardboard tube. If you're a TP aficionado like myself, you may try to convert the TP minority to your "*right*" way of thinking by espousing the virtues of TP over the top. Try comments like, "*Look how easy it is to grab when it's over the top*" or, "*Look how easy it is to make a TP triangle for your guests when it's over the top.*" If all else fails, leave a copy of my poem, *"TP Goes Over the Top"* on their stash of Charmin.

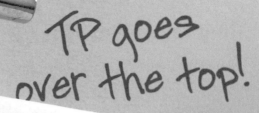

TP goes over the top!

What is with this issue?
The debate needs to stop.
Everyone should know the rule by now.
Toilet paper goes over the top!

It's hard to make a change,
but try it if you please.
When TP is over the top,
you can grab it with greater ease.

Your guests will really thank you,
your company will be impressed—
not scrambling underneath,
becoming all distressed.

Please do me a favor,
at least give it a chance.
You'll really like the change,
and cleaner underpants!

They Know Not What They Do

I remember dating a guy once (ONCE) who blew his nose into a cloth napkin. It was as if the record on the jukebox screeched to a halt (some of you younger readers have no idea what I'm talking about). Is there a rule against the cloth napkin nose blow? YES!!! Stunned, I looked at him and asked what he was doing and his big reply was, *"They wash them."* What?! Are you kidding me? I was mortified. It was over. He told me I have way too many rules. Yes I do, and he didn't know any of them. NEXT!

What do we do in this world of rule breakers? NOTHING. They don't need fixing (well, okay some of them do). What we can control is our response to their annoying habits. Listen, all these little things that bug you can add up to big things.

This creates disharmony in the workplace, in your relationships and in your day-to-day activities. So here's what you can do to help manage the stress that these rule breakers create in your life. Since you don't know what people are going through, make something up. Create a story about the rule-breaker's past. Don't tell anyone the story... it's just for you!

Make Up a Story

If people don't use their turn signals, don't get irritated. Instead say, *"Oh they didn't have enough money to get that option on their car!"* or *"Bummer, out of turn signal fluid!"*

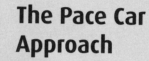

The Pace Car Approach

My family is familiar with the *"story"* idea. Last Christmas, my brother and I were driving, when some oblivious woman pulled in front of us and started going 10 mph below the speed limit. I was about to get crazy, when my brother looked at me and said, *"Pace Car."* Perfect!

Peace, Love & Understanding

Most people do NOT need your criticism and anger. They need your encouragement, support and prayers. I repeat: ENCOURAGEMENT, SUPPORT AND PRAYERS. It's tough out there for many people, so don't be too quick to judge. The bottom line is that hurt people want to hurt people. Loved people want to love people. Someone may have gotten in an accident recently, lost a loved one or been laid off. A rude customer service rep may have just gotten chewed out by his boss. And some people are just plain clueless about social behaviors. You just don't know! Now here's the bonus: if you give some stupid rule breaking person a pass, maybe, just maybe, when you do something stupid, someone will give you a pass when you need it most!

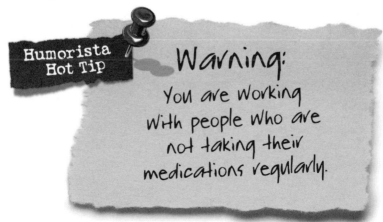

Humorista Hot Tip

Warning: You are working with people who are not taking their medications regularly.

High Tide Will Return

Typically, we are harder on ourselves than anybody else. I remember one month in particular where I kept losing things and driving myself (and everyone around me) crazy. I couldn't leave the house without coming back inside three more times. *"Oh, my sun glasses," "Better bring some water," "Where's the bag of Cheerios?"* It was a disaster. Have you ever misplaced something and blamed the people you live with, only to find what you were missing in that OTHER place where you laid it down?

During this bout of forgetfulness, I decided to phone a friend. *"Mary – I think there's something wrong with me, I'm misplacing, forgetting and losing things constantly and am losing my mind in the process."* She wisely replied, *"Honey, it's okay. You're having a low-tide day."* What? A low-tide day? She continued, *"You know – it's when things float out with the tide. Don't worry, Christine. In a few days, high tide will come in and bring everything back!"* I love that! Have you ever had a low-tide day, week or month? Everything eventually floats back.

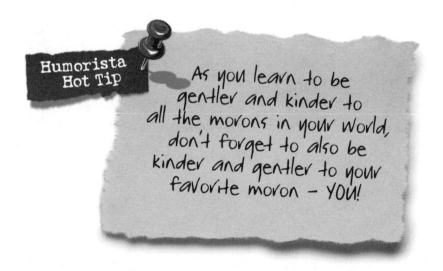

Humorista Hot Tip

As you learn to be gentler and kinder to all the morons in your world, don't forget to also be kinder and gentler to your favorite moron – YOU!

The Good Stuff

2

Why Can't Everyone Just Get Along?

Have you been subjected to those personality profiles before? The Shapes? DISC? The Colors? Myers-Briggs? The Ice Cream Flavors? If you haven't, there are some really great tools out there that help us learn tons about ourselves and others in our lives.

So why is it important to understand different personality types? Because so often, it feels like everyone is speaking a different language! Why is that? Because our brains are wired so differently. Take it from someone who married an engineer, it can be extremely frustrating to communicate!

Who Are You?? I Really Wanna Know!

Let's start by blending all of those personality tests together so we can learn how to better understand each other. The four basic personality types are: Who, Why, How, What and WHATEVER. Wait... that's five... but we're not going to talk about those apathetic WHATEVER people.

The Who People

Now, WHO people are easy to identify. They're *"people"* people. They're warm, personable and seem to know everyone. They're connected. They bring people together and love to create harmony.

"Who's happy? Who's stressed? Whose birthday is it? It's your birthday? We're singing at 10 o'clock. Are you mad at me? You know I've got candy in my desk... want some?" Favorite line: *"I don't care, what do you want to do?"*

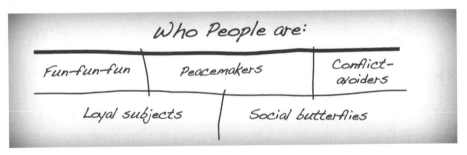

Who People are:

Fun-fun-fun	Peacemakers	Conflict-avoiders
Loyal subjects		Social butterflies

The Why People

WHY people are curious and creative types. Their minds are always working and they're always challenging the status quo, in an attempt to make things better and innovate.

"Why not? Why don't we do it this way? Why don't we do it that way? If it ain't broke, break it!" They're the people who see the **Road Closed** sign and think, it looks good to me! Favorite line: *"Just change the deadline. What's one more day, people – it's not brain surgery."*

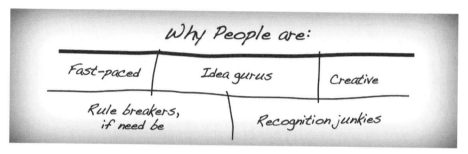

Why People are:

| Fast-paced | Idea gurus | Creative |

Rule breakers, if need be   Recognition junkies

The What People

WHAT people are the drivers. If you want something done, get a WHAT person to head-up the team. They are leaders, charging forward and accomplishing many tasks in a single bound. They rarely delegate. Why? By the time they explain the task to some moron, they could have done it themselves – and done it far better!

"What do you want? What do you need? What's happening? Cut to the chase. Move over and let the big dog drink!" Favorite line: *"What's the bottom line?"*

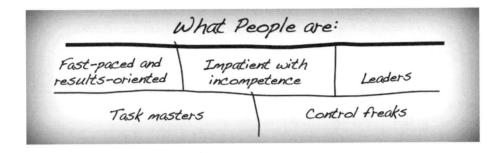

What People are:

Fast-paced and results-oriented	Impatient with incompetence	Leaders
Task masters		Control freaks

The How People

HOW people are the linear thinkers – detail oriented and accurate. They are well organized, hate to be wrong, are sticklers for precision and hate group hugs. If you want something done right, get a HOW person.

"How long is it going to take? How much is it going to cost? How is that possible?" Favorite line: *"Get real."*

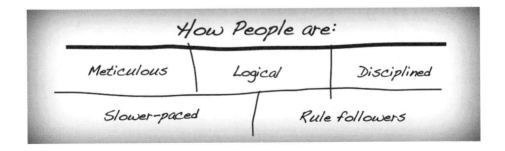

How People are:

Meticulous	Logical	Disciplined
Slower-paced		Rule followers

Who Are YOU? and Who Are THEY? Figure out which personality type you are. Then identify the personality types for the 5 people you hang out with the most.

Me	Who	Why	What	How
1. ___				
2. ___				
3. ___				
4. ___				
5. ___				

Identifying Your Fellow Shoppers

Can you see yourself in one of these categories? Most people are dominant in one area, but many of us are combo platters – with characteristics from a few personality types. See if you can identify yourself in the following scenario: You're at the grocery store. The lines are SO long.

A WHAT person would say, *"What's going on here? Excuse me, manager – could we get another lane open here?"*

The WHY people consider the fact that there are 27 check-out lanes but only 3 are open. They have the bright idea to open another lane, but instead of telling the manager, they get everybody completely riled up contemplating, *"Why?"*

Meanwhile, the WHO people are chatting everyone up in line. *"Can you believe this line? WOW, yellow is a fabulous color on you. It's fantastic!"*

Then you have the HOW people in the express line.

What do you think they're doing? Yes, they're counting the items in everyones' baskets, making sure there's not a violator in the line.

The Skinny on All These Crazy Personalities

The bad news is that working with all these different communication styles can be challenging. The good news is that we need each other. We need the WHAT people to get the job done. We also need the WHO people to keep morale high. We need the good WHY ideas, and we need the HOW people to pull the details together.

It's Not All About You

The key to all this personality profiling and communication is... drum roll here... to get along you must speak in the other person's language. It doesn't matter what your style is. It's not about you. If you want to be successful, speak their language!

Here's how it works: You're a WHAT person, so you might approach someone with, *"Hey – what's up? What's going on? Here's what we need."*

But wait! You're talking to a WHO person, so you better go to Whoville ASAP. If you use the WHAT approach, you may get a response like this: *"Excuse me. Could I get a good morning?"* *"Someone didn't get coffee!"* WHO people need the warm-up. Even if it isn't your style, do it anyway! *"Yes. Oh, my gosh –*

I can't believe May is here either. It really is amazing. All right. Here's what I need." If you're dealing with a WHO person, start with a little conversation and social bonding. In short order, your WHO person will be ready to listen to what you have to say.

The WHY people need to know "*why*." Even if it's none of their business (especially if it's none of their business!), they need to know the "*why*" before they buy. HOW people need the details. And, with a WHAT person, cut to the chase. Start with, *"Here's what's going on,"* and watch their ears perk up. Yes! Productivity, baby!

Again, speak in their language! When I want to get my HOW guy in a romantic mood, I say, *"Honey – would you make me an Excel Spreadsheet?"* I know. TMI – but it works!

Change for Change

Do you ever feel like you are the only competent human in the entire world? It's easy to find fault with everything and everyone. And sure, maybe you can do many things far better than most, but unless you want to live on a desert island alone, knock it off! Not only does this negative attitude create stress for you, it's a total downer for everyone in your life. So here's a great hot tip for taking off your *"critical contacts"* and putting something positive on your peepers. We all know it's about perspective and how we see the world, right? Well, here's change you can believe in (without the politics).

Take the *"Ten Coin Challenge."* When you get dressed, put 10 coins in your left pocket (yes, wear pockets) and begin your day looking for something good to comment on. I know! This may be difficult, but do it anyway.

Tell your partner how much you appreciated finding the newspaper on the kitchen table. Thank your kids for getting themselves up on time. Now here's the change part... each time you appreciate someone, move a coin from your left pocket to your right. Please be subtle so no one knows what you're doing. *"Hey Sue, you look nice today... okay, coin in right pocket...."*

By the end of the day, you should have all the coins in your right pocket. Full coin transfer may not happen every day, but if you get in the habit of looking through your half-full glasses, you'll definitely notice your attitude and attitudes of those around you shifting in a positive way. When you look for the good, you will find it more often, and of course the reverse works as well.

For advanced readers, if you catch yourself whipping out a negative non-constructive comment, move a coin back to your left pocket. If you come to the end of the day with a complete deficit, then you may want to seek a new job or take some courses in anger management. All I'm saying is give change a chance — it makes sense (get it?).

Difficult People

It doesn't matter what group I speak to – accountants, truckers, dog trainers – whenever I talk about difficult people, I instantly see that look of recognition in peoples' eyes.

Yes. We work with these people. We grew up with these people. These people are somehow in customer service positions (don't get me started!).

We may even LIVE with these people. Difficult people are everywhere and they take up our time and drain our energy. Often times, just talking about them brings up a whole slew of emotions and even physical changes in our bodies. In fact, my long ago *"boss from hell"* just popped into my brain and my stomach did a flip. The sad part is that I'm pretty sure he isn't thinking about me.

We need to move on! Men are great at this. Juan will get into an argument with David and 5 minutes later plan a golf outing – yes – with David, the same guy he just swore was the biggest jerk in the entire world. I love you dudes for this! Women, on the other hand, do not forget. In fact, we may not even remember what the issue was; we just don't like the person and know it was **something.**

12:00

12:05

We Shall Overcome

If we would all just speak the truth more (in the right way, of course), there would be far more peace, love and harmony in everyday life. One of my favorite childhood songs from church was, *"Let there be peace on earth and let it begin with me..."* But sometimes keeping the peace can be a challenge when so many people seem hell bent on bugging you – but you can overcome!

Now to overcome is going to take some stealth and vigor. Why you ask? Because difficult people, like ice cream, come in many flavors. So read on and you'll learn to identify and deal with the different flavors of difficult people in your life.

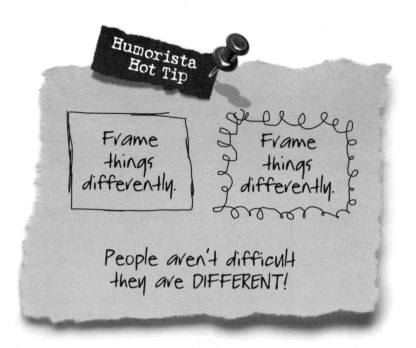

Frame things differently.

Frame things differently.

People aren't difficult they are DIFFERENT!

"I Don't Care... What Do You Want to Do?"

Lambs. You know who they are. So nice. So easy-going. Everyone likes them. But SO annoying if you're trying to make plans or get their true opinions! Lambs are very non-confrontational and rarely if ever speak up about what they think or feel, so as not to make waves. Truth be told: these people care a lot! Here is a typical conversation with Passive Polly...

26 | www.ChristineCashen.com

And they do have wants and needs. But they rarely express them because they are so eager to please and have such a great need for approval. But warning Will Robinson: these simmering tea kettles, given enough time and pressure, may explode.

So if you have a Passive Polly in your life who makes you crazy, encourage her (and it may take a lot of encouragement) to give you true opinions about wants and desires. Tell Polly that today she is deciding where you will have lunch. End of story.

I Hate Bullies

At school. At work. At home. Yes, aggressive people are everywhere. Tell me about aggressive people. TELL ME! *"If I want your opinion, I'll give it to you."* These people like to bully and manipulate others. Unfortunately, aggressive people are often rewarded – because they get what they want! Please don't reward them by giving in. Why? Because if they are jerky and then get what they want, it will just encourage even more jerky-ness!

So how do you deal with Aggressive Andy? While your first inclination may be to fight fire with fire and be aggressive right back, typically that only makes matters worse. Remember: Do not fight back! I repeat: Do not fight back!

Instead, try being that cool water in the face of fire. First thing to remember: don't take ANYTHING Aggressive Andy says personally (he can't help it – he was raised by a pack of wolves). Simply stand your ground in a calm cool way and work to bring the conversation to focus on the issue at hand – not the person. Talk Andy down. Even bullies need to be loved and understood. Keep in mind that hurt people want to hurt people. So try to understand where your Andy is coming from by searching for the kernel of truth in his words and working toward resolution. Again... water on fire.

Does this strategy always work? Of course not! Sometimes the situation is just too intense and emotional. So DEFUSE! Try this exit line. It works every time: *"Andy... you deserve respect from me but I can't give it to you right now. Let's take a break and discuss this later."*

When Passive Polly Meets Aggressive Andy... WATCH OUT!

When these two meet, the result may be a beautiful love child but this passive-aggressive pain-in-the-rear has no social skills whatsoever. Here's how this works:

Some people make friends like this! In fact, some people think organizational teambuilding means you all hate the same person together. That's not teambuilding! That's team destruction. Find a new way of pulling together other than, *"Can you believe she did that?"*

So how do you deal with a Lucy? First make sure it isn't you. As ugly as this looks, take a hard look at your own behavior as this gossipy-let's-hate-her-together scenario is more common than you might think.

If you're on the receiving end of complaints or gossip, as Dan is with Lucy, the best strategy is to send the person back to the source. So if Lucy approached Dan to complain about Pat demanding numbers, Dan might redirect Lucy's energy to a place where it can make a difference by saying, *"Well, did you talk to Pat about your deadline concerns?"*

It's All in the Delivery

Speak the truth and be assertive. **Say what you mean. Mean what you say. Do you know the next part? Don't be mean when you say it.** How you say it is everything. This is especially true of those people who are from the South. I grew up in the gorgeous state of Michigan, lived in Chicago, then San Francisco and now reside in the great state of

Texas. This is where I got my *"Southern education."* Southerners can say anything and with that kindly Southern drawl, anything and everything comes out just fine. Picture a Southern belle, fanning herself in the summer heat, saying sweetly, *"Well, dahlin'... you can just go to hell,"* and the recipient would smile and thank her for the suggestion.

There's also the *dig-followed-by-love* approach. It goes like this: *"Did you see Caroline's outfit? Wasn't that just awful? Bless her heart!"* Why does this work? Because if you bless the heart of this poor girl with such bad taste, you can say any nasty thing you want. It really is a phrase used by Southern women to excuse them for speaking ill of others – and it works!

Silk Purses into Sows' Ears

If you have to deal with some or any of these crazy behaviors in your life, the first step may be to approach the situation differently, especially if what you're doing now isn't working! Try a few of these:

1. Deal with it – the sooner the better – so it doesn't fester.

2. Become a fact finder. Ask questions to get to the bottom of the behavior: *"You seem really upset by this... please tell me why."*

3. Really LISTEN. Frequently, we are plotting a response in our heads when we should be paying close attention to what's being said at the present moment.

4. Find a point of agreement. What is it that you CAN agree on and let that be the starting point for your discussion: *"I think we'd agree that the objective is to support the students...."*

5. The "I"s have it. Speak in "I" language rather than "you" language. Instead of, *"You always interrupt me during meetings,"* try, *"I find it difficult to make my point when interrupted."*

6. Give up the need to be right all the time. I know, just breathe through this one. Say, *"You might be right, let me think about it."* The conversation will take a new course.

7. Spin it positive. Instead of, *"You never clean your room,"* use, *"You have yet to clean your room."*

8. Watch your language. Instead of saying, *"I disagree with you,"* explain, *"I see things differently."*

9. Be willing to compromise. *"What do we need to do to get through this?"*

10. Script what you want to say before you have the discussion.

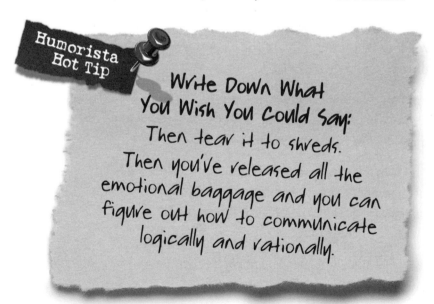

Humorista Hot Tip

Write Down What You Wish You Could Say: Then tear it to shreds. Then you've released all the emotional baggage and you can figure out how to communicate logically and rationally.

The Good Stuff

3

When Work Is Whacked

From Brain Drain to Brain Hurricane

There's nothing worse than sitting around a meeting table, staring at stale bagels and being tasked with BRAINSTORMING! Most brainstorms are mere drizzles at best. Everyone sits, waiting for an idea to strike like lightning, and of course, it rarely does.

So you pull all your courage together, break the silence with an amazing idea, and what do you hear? *"We've tried that before and it didn't work,"* or, *"Where would we get the money/resources?"* or my favorite and the ever-popular, *"Oh, you must be new here."* Enough!

Organizations run the gamut in terms of fostering creativity. I have a friend who claims that creativity in her office died years ago. Yet other organizations love to foster new ideas and innovative thinking. Still others may look on new ideas as a threat to the status quo.

From HA-HA to AH-HA

Creativity hates stress. The best ideas come when your mind is relaxed. So get your team laughing, joking and NOT judging. There is a direct link between the *"AH-HA"* moment, when a great idea lands in your brain and the *"HA-HA"* of laughter. So have fun with brainstorming. Caffeine, funny hats and clown noses really do work. And often the best ideas come when piggybacking on someone else's ridiculous one. When people are enjoying what they do, there is a better chance of coming up with a great idea. The innovative brain locks down during stress. Lighten up and let the good ideas roll!

So ONE MORE TIME: ABSOLUTELY NO PREMATURE JUDGING of ideas. Judging stops the creative flow in a heartbeat. There are three times to judge an idea: Now, Later and Never. Assessing the validity of the idea needs to happen, but L-A-T-E-R.

Humorista's Top 10
Idea Generation Locations

10 On the potty

9 Working out

8 When you're supposed to be doing something else

7 At 4 a.m.

6 While supposedly listening to your boss or spouse

5 Driving on auto-pilot

4 Collaborating with another fun person

3 In the shower

2 Daydreaming

1 Just before sleepy time (z-z-z-z-z)

Putting the Storm into Brainstorming

If you want to jump on the fast-track to AMAZING ideas, play the *"What If"* game. Just follow these simple rules:

1. Bring everyone together with a pen and paper (all ideas are good so no pencils and no erasers). And don't sit in the same seat you always sit in!

2. Set the timer for 5 minutes.

3. Everyone has to come up with 25 ideas – good, bad and *"pie in the sky"* are all good! Think inside and outside and on the dark side of the box! It's about quantity, not quality at this point. Say it with me now... *"NO JUDGING!"*

4. Assign someone to record the best ideas on a white board.

5. Everyone yell out your Top 5 Ideas.

6. Now start deciding which ones are best. And remember, don't be mean. Talk about the ideas you like, not the ones you don't. And remember, sometimes the crazy ideas are just crazy enough to work!

Don't be a meanie!
Ideas are just like little babies.
Some are cuter than others,
but all deserve your love and respect!

Don't Let Those Great Ideas Escape!

Have you ever had a great idea right before sleepy time and thought,
"I really should write that down. Naaa, I'll remember in the morning."
And POOF, you wake up the next morning and the thought has magically
disappeared. Whether you jot them down on a pad beside your bed,
leave yourself a voice mail message or slap a sticky note on your computer
monitor, the trick is to capture these ideas as
they happen, because you will NEVER
get them back. Try taking an *"idea spin."*
Every time you get a great idea,
write it down in your Rolodex
and the next time you're stumped,
just take a spin and get inspired.

Ok, You've got like one minute to write me down - then I'm outta here!

Great Idea

From Brain Drain to Breakthrough Thinking

Creativity is like a muscle that you flex. So warm it up before you work it out – especially if it's been awhile. If you're in a creative rut, a quick break from your old habits may be just the ticket....

- Change your morning routine – (make sure someone checks you out before you leave the house)

- Wear your watch on the opposite hand

- Take a different route to work

- Doodle or write with your non-dominant hand

- Get an opinion from a total stranger

- Ask a kid – you may be surprised at the answer!

Warm up your creative brain by coming up with solutions to everyday irritations

A GPS tracker for your TV remote?

A self-cleaning bathtub?

What can YOU come up with?

Are You Sitting Next to Someone Who Retired Years Ago... Mentally?

A creative bug can be contagious – so can apathy! There are far too many people who retire, and they don't tell anybody! I bet you know some. Maybe you're sitting right next to one. They keep coming to work every day, being miserable, doing mediocre work and taking up space. You'll know you've spotted an apathy Queen when you hear her say, *"That's not my job."* One of my BFFs and talented songwriter/speaker, Jana Stanfield says, *"Don't take up space in someone else's dream job."* Isn't that great?! Find your passion people!!

Many of us are on auto pilot, into the same routine day-after-day, month-after-month, year-after-year. Mix it up! It doesn't matter what your job is. Find a way to put your heart into it! We've all run into people who exhibit passion in unlikely professions. My personal favorite is the highway toll taker who is dancing in her booth and giving people a huge smile during each transaction. Don't you feel better after coming in contact with people who are having fun?

The Show Must Go On

So I'm at the grocery store and the cashier checking me out spent the entire transaction complaining about her job to the cashier in the next aisle. And she went on to say that she didn't care what the boss thought about her leaving early. HUH? The irony: she wore this huge button that said, *"I CARE."*

Everyone is entitled to an off day, but that doesn't mean you should be broadcasting it to everyone within earshot. One summer during college, I worked at Walt Disney World in Florida. One of the great training tips I learned that summer was that when you are at work, you're *"on stage."* You leave your troubles at the door and play your part to perfection. Could you imagine seeing Mickey Mouse hanging out in front of the Disney gates, costume head off, taking a smoke break? If you aren't *"on stage"* for your job, you probably won't dash the dreams of children like a smoking Mickey, but your behavior on-the-job makes a strong impression. Someone is PAYING you to represent your organization well, which gives you great power to damage or enhance your employer's reputation. Remember... you represent your employer at all times, and yes, even on your break.

It's a Small (and Annoying) World

That Disney summer, I worked at the *It's a Small World* ride. Can you imagine listening to that song over and over and over and over? Oh great, now it's running through my head. It's probably running through your head now too. Sorry about that.

Anyway, I'm sure you can imagine how challenging it could be to the spirit some days. To make life tolerable on the tough days, I would try to pick out kids who looked a little sad or parents who looked a little frazzled and do something extra special to make them happy. Of course this was part of the job description – *"to make some magic"* – but some days were MUCH harder than others. I found that *"high-fives"* were often a blues buster as guests were passing me in their boats. It was the best when I could get the older people on the boat to give me *"high-fives"* as well. Some days I'd even whip a clown nose out of my pocket, place it on my schnoz and try to remain serious while asking, *"How many in your party?"* It always brought smiles. The biggest one was always mine.

Get Down and BOOGIE-OOGIE-OOGIE!

Ever have one of those days where you have no energy, your cubicle feels like a jail cell, your co-workers are clueless and EVERYTHING is getting on your last nerve? Listen, I know we all have our down days. If you've ever felt down, blue and full blown cranky, guess what?! You're HUMAN. Congratulations! I swear, every time I see commercials on TV asking, *"Are you tired? Listless? Have trouble concentrating? Trouble getting out of bed?"* I'm positive that millions of people, just like me, are yelling at their televisions, *"YES! YES! YES!"*

Sure sometimes medication is called for. On the other hand, you may not need to drop everything and run immediately to your doc for a prescription. For most of us, being tired and cranky is part of being

Learn the BOOGIE Dance!

Be!

fig. 1

Outstanding!

fig. 2

human, with too many commitments and too little time. We're all busy! The trick, of course, is to have more highs than lows, more good days than bad. So here's the plan. To make sure you have more happy days, you have to BOOGIE as much as you can. Some of you are already grabbing dancing shoes, but just hold on! BOOGIE is an acronym for **B**e **O**utstanding **O**r **G**et **I**nvolved **E**lsewhere!

To truly BOOGIE, you must know the BOOGIE dance. Okay, now it's time to get those dancing shoes. Are you ready?

So you say... you're in a dead-end job. Your boss is a whack-job. Your children are delinquent, and your spouse thinks romance is getting your car tires rotated. So how do you BOOGIE in that situation? Just look at the offending person square in the eye, do the BOOGIE dance, then keep on walkin'... you don't want to catch what he has!

fig. 3

fig. 4

Humorista's Top 10
Tips for Learning to BOOGIE

10 Find one thing about your job where you can make a difference and DO IT!

9 Have an attitude of gratitude

8 Identify your passion and find a way to make a living from it

7 Try a little harder

6 Learn something new every day

5 Get a mentor and be a mentor

4 Volunteer

3 Choose happiness

2 Decide to make a difference

1 If you can't change your SITUATION, then CHANGE your situation

Go on a Secret Mission

So you're having a great day – checking things off the list, returning phone calls, conquering e-mails, and generally calling PRODUCTIVITY your middle name. Then your co-worker, Ms. Donna Drama, comes in and insists on interrupting your groove with an impromptu 20-minute therapy session. WHAT?! So now how do you get your groove back? Here's what you do. Go on a Secret Mission – NOW! It's easy.

Step 1: Grab a folder or a clipboard. You have to have something in your hands. (In a pinch, blank copier paper will do. Just hold onto it with gusto!)

Step 2: Walk briskly for three minutes around the office. If your office is small, head outside and around the building. This is the tricky part. You have

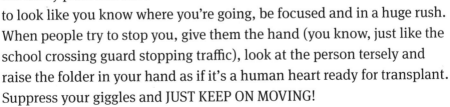

to look like you know where you're going, be focused and in a huge rush. When people try to stop you, give them the hand (you know, just like the school crossing guard stopping traffic), look at the person tersely and raise the folder in your hand as if it's a human heart ready for transplant. Suppress your giggles and JUST KEEP ON MOVING!

Step 3: After a good 2-3 minutes, go back to your desk, put your stuff down and declare, *"Mission accomplished!"* A mental break to a physical break is exactly what you may need to get your mojo back on track. Some of you have been going on these clandestine trips for a long time, but you didn't have a name for them. Well now you do!

So when things get rough... get up, get moving, get the blood flowing and you'll be back on track in no time at all!

Geeeeezzzz Man... It's a Secret!

If you see someone whiz by your desk, clipboard in hand, and you suspect a Secret Mission, KEEP IT QUIET! Don't bust co-workers on their missions. You never know when you may be on your own mission and need someone to cover for you. Or maybe you're having a bad day too? Grab your stuff and follow!

The Good Stuff

4

E-mails,
Telephones &
Other
Time Wasters

All Hail E-Mail

One of the best ways to communicate is via e-mail. It's the best because it's fast, easy and immediate. It's also one of the worst, because it may not be communicating what you think! Have you ever gotten a message from someone who ruffled your feathers so much that you crack your knuckles before pounding the keys in anger and belting out a hostile nasty-gram in reply? STOP! It's better to wait 24 hours before sending that message or even better, pick up the phone and call. You know that you may *"hear"* a tone of voice in what you read that may not have been intended. My mother used to send me messages in all CAPS. SHE WASN'T YELLING. SHE SAID IT WAS EASIER FOR HER TO TYPE THAT WAY. Did you hear yelling? I did too and asked her to stop.

Privacy? Come On!

Never write anything in an e-mail that you wouldn't want posted on a billboard. You never know who is forwarding your messages AND it may be used against you in a court of law. Seriously. Haven't you heard horror stories about this? A friend of mine was having difficulty with her employer because HR insisted on numerous copies of a doctor's note as explanation for her time off. She wrote the doctor and told him that she worked for morons and could he please fax another copy of her records to HR. The doctor did fax the copy to her employer, along with her e-mail about their being morons – yikes!

Just Say No to "Reply to All"

Don't you hate when people *"Reply to All"* unnecessarily? There's nothing more frustrating than going to your In Box to find a message that says, *"Thanks,"* or *"You're Welcome,"* or *"I agree."* Actually there is something more frustrating: the endless-cycle-reply-to-all-e-mail-extravaganza! Here's how it works. It's 5 p.m. You're ready to leave. Everything's in great order and suddenly your In Box is populated with messages from a bunch of people you don't even know. One message says, *"Stop replying to all,"* and the next one says, *"What HE said,"* and the one after that says, *"Ditto."*

What's going on here? Everyone is replying to all and the e-mails are multiplying like little bunnies! Don't add to the chaos by replying to all with, *"Stop replying to all."* Write back to the person directly. We all get way too many irrelevant messages as it is, so think really hard before typing, *"Reply to All."*

Humorista Hot Tip

Don't forward anything unless it's fall-on-the-floor funny!

But wait – there's more. Hold on while I jump on my soapbox again. Please stop forwarding any warnings unless you have checked them out at www.snopes.com, so you aren't guilty of circulating panic for no reason. Same goes for the, *"You will have bad luck if you don't send this to 37 other people in the next 14 minutes."* Hey man, I don't need the extra pressure or spam. ONLY when something is killer funny or fall off your chair hysterical, should you contemplate forwarding. Do you really want to be one of those people who gets the rep for sending stupid e-mail? Your friends will start deleting your e-mails before they even open them... *"Oh, another one from Kelly. I'm sure it's more junk."* Stop this. Chances are, your friends have seen these e-mails already.

Oh and one more thing... getting an e-mail from a long lost friend or relative only to find out it's a stupid forwarded message that she's sent to 30 other people is such a let down. Don't do this. The only forwarded stuff I want to receive is from friends and family who I hear from on a regular basis.

"I'm Either on the Other Line or Away from my Desk"

Duh! No kidding. Change your voice mail greeting. If your greeting says, *"I'm either on the other line or away from my desk,"* give me a break. Who started this greeting? I'm going to find her and slap her. What's irritating about voice mail and what wastes your precious time is when people leave numbers that are completely unintelligible. *"Please call me at nineseventwothreetwonineoblahbzzzer."* What? You have to listen to the message 10 times so you can get one digit each time. Even more frustrating is when people leave a name and you can't understand it. Then you have to call back and fake that you know who you are calling. *"Is ummm Fa-Fa there?"* It is especially ineffective if you don't know when to call back and don't know why the person called.

Humorista Hot Tip

Change Your Voice Mail Greeting

Help people help you by changing your voice mail greeting. Ask for these 4 elements:

- Their name
- Their number – s l o w l y
- The nature of their call
- A good time to reach them

Quick warning: Upon hearing your new greeting your ding dong friends will call and leave their numbers much too slowly just to irritate you, *"niiiiiiinnnnnneeeeeeee sevennnnnnnnn twoooooooooooo,"* but at least you get all of the numbers. Don't forget to review your new message after you record it. One time I called an air-conditioning company and this was the

greeting: *"Thank you for callin' Big Dave's Air-Conditionin' and Coolin' aw hell... BEEP!"* Dave must've gotten interrupted while changing his greeting, botched it and didn't remember to go back and fix it. I actually had to call back to leave my message. I was so dumbfounded the first time I called, that I had to hang up and get all my giggles out!

Where Did My Day Go?

Have you ever made your to-do list only to find that at the end of your crazy busy day, you didn't accomplish one single item on that list? Then, do you write down what you did do so you can then cross it all off and feel like you accomplished something? Me too! Sometimes you just need to feel a sense of completion. I remember going to a time management seminar and the leader explained that everyone should keep a time log. Who has time for that?! Here are some quick ideas that will help you get a handle on your day.

Worker Interrupted

It is so frustrating when people come into your workspace with, *"You gotta minute?"* and you know it's never a minute. The obvious thing to do is to ask, *"What's up?"* BEFORE you commit to giving this person your precious time. It depends on what she wants, right?!

If your visitor just wants to chat about the latest *People* Magazine cover or the game last night, you need to parrot this question, *"What can I help you with?"* over and over to find out what work-related thing he may need. This is really great for those social interrupters who use you as their break time. Another thing you can do is stand up. Even though you have nowhere to go, it will create a sense of urgency in the other person. Whatever you do, don't let her sit down. Ugh! You will add an extra 12 minutes to the conversation – at least!

Interrupted Log

Keep a log of who interrupts you with just the initials written down. Why does this person keep coming in? Is it purely social? Or does she need information or help on a project? Logging will show you who the time stealers are and if their reasons are legit. Maybe you need to provide better information to your subordinates when you delegate, or perhaps a good heart-to-heart about the social visits needs to happen. Be glad that you are so approachable, and at the same time, try to put a stop to repeat time-stealing offenders.

When you do get interrupted, make the person wait for a second (unless it's your boss) and put a quick sticky note on your work so that it's easier to come back to it. Having your visitor witness your application of said sticky note tells the time-stealer that YES YOU WERE in the middle of something critically important. The next step is to look up at your intruder, bright-eyed and still entranced by the work you were just FORCED to put off due to this terrible interruption and say, *"So what can I help you with?"*

This person should get the message: CUT TO THE CHASE. Tell me what it is and get out! I have important work to do. Oh yeah... another advantage to sticky notes holding your place... if you win the lotto and don't come back, someone knows where you left off.

Prioritize: A, B, C THIS...

If you've ever been to a time management course, you know that they tell you to prioritize by letters. A is urgent, B is almost urgent and C is something to do when you get a moment. Too often all of us do the C tasks first. Why? Because they're easy. They allow you to check something off the list and feel some sense of accomplishment. The more important A and B tasks may get arrowed to the following day – especially if they contain undesirable tasks. Do the thing you don't want to do FIRST and get it DONE. Have you ever put something off only to discover that once you did it, it wasn't so bad and you wasted more time worrying about it than doing it? Tackle it pronto so that you can get your mojo working through the rest of the items.

Meeting Overload

We've all sat through meetings that take WAY too much time and accomplish WAY too little. How many times have you thought, *"Geeeeezzz, if we didn't have so many meetings, I could actually get some work done!"*

Try the PALS Method to Cut Down on Your Meeting Craziness:

P = Know the **Purpose** of the meeting well in advance. Have concrete goals and objectives and just because it's Monday (we always have staff meetings on Monday, right?) doesn't count.

A = Have an **Agenda** and actually follow it.

L = Find a creative way to **Limit** the time people can talk. One company I know of actually had people anonymously knock under the table if someone got off topic to tell the speaker to get back on task.

S = **Start** and **Stop** on time. Get creative! Late person to the meeting has to take the meeting minutes. If you are late, you must bring snacks to the next meeting. Anyone who is late must stand for the rest of the meeting – no chairs. In fact, some companies are holding *"standing meetings"* where participants actually stand the entire meeting. They have found that the meeting time is cut in half when people can't sit back in a comfy chair.

Have a Block Party

Do your tasks in blocks of time. Rather than respond to an e-mail here, take a call there, file a bit here and inject a, *"Do you gotta minute?"* there, get a grip on your schedule before your day unproductively flies by.

Avoid jumping on e-mail first thing. I know it's hard because there is an inbox brimming with exciting news and information, but it can wait. Are there other true priorities? Let those e-mails ride, then jump on and ride the wave for an allotted amount of time. Respond, delete, respond, delete and delete. Then close out. Make  all your calls in one fell swoop. Spend a chunk of time working through the paper mountain. Consider a daily *"door-shut"* hour between 2-3 p.m. where you can work on tasks that require great concentration. You can even train your co-workers that this is your *"power hour"* and you are not to be interrupted. Sure someone will knock on your door at 2:15, but try saying kindly, *"Can this wait til 3? I'm in the middle of THE most important document in the world!"* Without a doubt, you will get more done when you get your groove on conquering one block of tasks at a time, rather than working in segmented parts.

Go Home and Be Free

Don't wait until morning to write out your to-do list. Write it at the end of your day instead. This will create a sense of closure and also a launching point for the next day. Put a sticky note on what you were doing last or what is on deck for the morning. You won't have to struggle with the *"Where was I?"* dilemma the next day. It may also help you crazies out there (I'm in that group too) who sit bolt upright in the middle of the night with the sudden realization that you should've done something the day before. To make sure that you don't forget again, you call yourself at work and leave a voicemail. The next morning you hear this caller with a scratchy voice reminding you to send the FedEx to Brownsville. While pondering who this mystery caller is, you come to the realization (and horror) that it was YOU calling at 4 a.m.

Say Good Night to Your Piles

Arrange your papers and piles neatly before you walk out of the office to go home. Look back at your desk and tell your work, "You stay here, I will see you tomorrow." This will prevent your subconscious from working throughout the night!

Homework

For those of you who work from home, there may be fewer meetings to contend with, but without a doubt there are other HUGE distractions. Sometimes it's the little things that throw you over the edge. Whether it's the pictures that suddenly call to you to be straightened, deciding what to make for dinner or a friendly neighbor coming over (there goes an hour!), the same time management strategies and a whole lot of discipline are key.

The Good Stuff

5

I Love My Family, But...

Know What You Sign Up For...

My mother decided that my dad needs to be more romantic. I remind her of his proposal over 40 years ago: *"See if this ring will fit your chubby finger...."* Can you believe she said *"Yes!?"* Do you know how close I am to not existing?

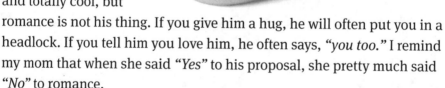

My dad is a truly wonderful man. He is witty, reliable, honest and totally cool, but romance is not his thing. If you give him a hug, he will often put you in a headlock. If you tell him you love him, he often says, *"you too."* I remind my mom that when she said *"Yes"* to his proposal, she pretty much said *"No"* to romance.

Pick the right partner and spouse without thinking that you will change him/her. Put your energy into getting what you want, rather than becoming a nag. We know this right? Guess who I married? The hottie engineer. To get him excited, I ask him to make me an Excel Spreadsheet. He makes my father's headlock look romantic. Accept what you cannot change... oh whatever, you know what I'm trying to say.

You can't change people. So learn to appreciate the qualities that first attracted you to your partner.

PERSONAL LIFE SPREADSHEET

A	B	C
Let's	Date night	My turn
go to	tonight –	to make
the park	no excuses!	dinner.
this		
weekend.		

Forget Jerry Maguire...
Complete Your Own D*** Self!

Let's talk about Jerry. Remember the line, *"You complete me."* Well get over it! The amazingly handsome, romantic men in the movies are just that: IN THE MOVIES. And guess why they are so romantic? Because the writers are good – and probably women!

There is the occasional romantic man and lucky is the woman who has him, but for the rest of us, we must create it for ourselves.

So what to do? You must complete yourself! If you want flowers, go get some! This way you get roses if you want roses and not what he decides lasts the longest or is on sale.

Don't be afraid to take yourself on a date. You are the only one you have sometimes and you need to learn to create your own happiness rather than wait for someone to bring it to you.

It **IS** All About You

Go to a great restaurant and ask for a table for two. If you ask for a table for one, you get the sympathy look and the crappiest seat in the house. When you ask for a table for two, you get a great seat up front and when the other person doesn't arrive, you get great sympathy service, and maybe a glass of wine on the house. Luckily, you happen to have your book with you so you can relax while someone serves you a yummy meal.

Get a Massage

I'm not talking about your significant other pushing on your shoulders for 5 minutes and petering out. I mean a professional massage. If people ask you what you want for your birthday, holiday or daylight savings time, tell them a massage gift certificate! Don't be shy. The first time I got a massage I was thinking, *"OMG this woman is squeezing my fat... HOLY COW... she's squeezing my fat!!!!"* And after five minutes, I was laying there in nirvana thinking, *"YES! KEEP SQUEEZING!"* Get over it. Massage therapists have seen it all and are not judging you. There are many health benefits to massage – go find out for yourself!

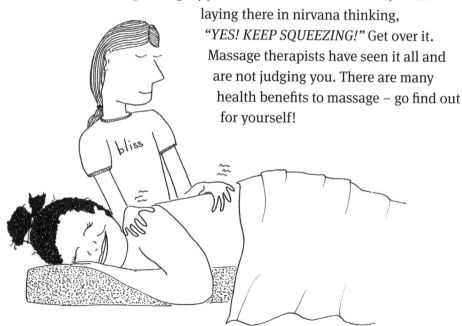

Wear Sexy Underwear Just For YOU

If you don't have any, go get some. There is nothing like spicing up your day with a leopard bra. And men, you can break out the funky boxers. Even making copies seems more exciting knowing that there is a party going on under your clothes. Stop judging and just go do it.

Asking For What You Want... AND GETTING IT!

My amazing yet crazy parents provide me with more material than I know what to do with. The scary thing is that I see myself exhibiting the same crazy behaviors after I promised myself that I would never EVER behave like that. So my mother (the small spunky Italian cutie) calls me the day before she and dad embark on their annual pilgrimage from Michigan to Florida. She sounds crazed. The call went something like this:

"Hi Mom"

"Hi honey"

"What's wrong?"

"It's your Father! We're getting ready to leave. I'm packing, cleaning, watering plants, getting everything ready, and what is your Father doing?????"

"Watching TV?"

"NO! Reading the paper!"

"Did you ask him to help?"

"HE SHOULD KNOW!" she hissed. "Can't he see me running around here like a maniac?"

Now, without even being there, I know exactly what's happened. My calm cool daddy sits patiently, reading the paper and trying to stay clear of the chaos while my manic mother rips around the house banging drawers and stomping past him with a glare that could easily burn a hole straight through his newspaper and directly into his brain. All the while, she thinks that he's going to get a clue.

He doesn't... or does he?

Over the course of their 40-year marriage, my Dad has in fact packed suitcases, loaded cars and watered plants. Mom's reaction to Dad's plant watering: *"How much water did you put in those plants?"* or *"Are you trying to kill them and ruin my carpet?"*

Regarding dad's packing, mom's reaction was, *"If you're wearing those ugly shorts from the '70s, you're walking alone!"*

My dad's no dummy. He knows that whatever it is he's tried in the past has been either (A) criticized (B) incorrect, or (C) done over by mom. So, he's decided that he'd rather take the heat of the *"glare"* than submit himself to critiques and insults.

Do Your Spoons Spoon?

Realize that sometimes *"good enough"* is good enough. Let it go! If you can't let it go, at least say something like, *"Honey, thanks for taking the garbage out. Hey, it would really help me if you could put the next liner in the can."* Don't be sarcastic but do provide more detail so that the next time the end result is closer to what you really want.

**You Have to Get a Clue...
Nobody Else Has One!**

Guess what? Most of the time, people have no freakin' clue what you want.

So it's up to you to ask for what you want, need and deserve!

I've pulled mom's martyr act on my husband only to realize that if I would just say, "Please help me get the kids dressed because we're late," he gladly would.

Warning! Warning! If you don't give up your perfectionistic ways, the people you live with will get the skinny rather quickly. For instance, maybe you live with someone who stacks dishes in the sink but has never contemplated the migration from sink to dishwasher. If you always load the dishwasher, why would anyone else bother? Let's get real. Are you one of those people who goes so far as to rearrange the silverware, so the spoons don't *"spoon?"* Why should anybody waste time when you are just going to embark on a silverware reorg?

Some powerful advice here: Let your spouse/son/sister put the spoons together! Let them hug, kiss, AND spoon. It's just not the end of the world. Dishwashers are pretty powerful these days and chances are, the spoons will come out pretty clean regardless. Celebrate the attempt. Work on the details later.

Who Named You King/Queen?

I know this may come as a huge surprise, but you aren't perfect either. Guess what I learned from my engineer hubby? That there is a right way to fold towels and sheets? Oh yes indeed. I didn't know about this. This is so embarrassing. A little background on me: I over-married. The guy's a saint. But we do have issues – he's an engineer. We can hardly make the bed together, because he's on the other side going,

"How much have you got on your side?"

Now back to folding sheets. He had to give me the tutorial. The man can fold a fitted sheet into a postage stamp. Just when I thought my corner-corner... oh, whatever, roll it in a ball and shove it in the linen closet *"technique"* was working just fine, I find out it bothers him.

So my first inclination is to dump the freshly dried towels and sheets on his lap while he's watching the Mavericks game. But I find that asking for his help and complimenting him on his amazing folding abilities works a lot better – for both of us!

The Humorista's (almost) Foolproof Guide to Getting Bees with Honey

When You'd LOVE to Say This...	Say This Instead...
Get your lazy bum off the couch and help me unload groceries.	Sweetheart...I've got 4 bags of groceries in the car. Could you help me unload? Then maybe we could spend some "quality time" upstairs.
Do you NOT see the pile of dirty, smelly clothes on the floor? Guess not...you've been walking around it for the past 5 days!	Sue is bringing her friend Lindsay home with her after school. Would you throw your underwear in the hamper before they get here?
You are such an idiot. We have $57 in fines for videos and most we didn't even watch!	Honey...I can't remember if I asked (OK...this IS a HUGE lie, but sometimes you gotta do what you gotta do) but could you return the videos on your way to work so we don't get a fine? I left them on top of your briefcase.
Isn't it great that the laundry fairy visits so often?	I need your help with something (they love this). You are so good at folding sheets and towels. Can you help me out?

Are You A Victim or A Volunteer?

Here's the scoop. We teach people how to treat us. It's like the time you're working diligently to get through the pile of papers and bills on your desk and your 12-year-old strolls in, plate and sandwich in hand, and says, *"Mom... can you cut the crusts off the sandwich for me?"*

"What??" He's 12. He made the sandwich. He walked up the steps. And of course he didn't even bring a knife! So you may be inclined to jump into your Supermom pose, *"I can fix that! I fix everything around here!"* You drop the bills on the desk, rush down to the kitchen and OFF WITH THE CRUST! Are YOU paying attention to you? No. Do you really want him calling from college 400 miles away, asking you to cut crust? I don't think so. Bottom line: often we're not the victims. We're the volunteers.

It's A BIG, FAT Lie!

Do you ever feel as though everyone has it together except you? Of course your neighbor down the street has a great marriage and four brilliant and amazingly well-adjusted children. She also works full-time, gets up every morning at 4 a.m. to go to the gym AND she has no body fat whatsoever. Did I mention that she's also PTO President, and single-handedly raises millions of dollars for cancer research every year? Well it's simply not true. There are only 24 hours in a day. Sure, some of us are fortunate enough to afford help or have a spouse who loves to cook, but for most of us, we're just doing our best to keep it together from one day to the next!

So what's with all the pressure? I sometimes think that women are preprogrammed to think that they can be everything to everybody these days. READ THIS: IT'S NOT POSSIBLE! All too often I hear friends say, *"I'm a bad mom..."* or, *"I should've done this, that or the other, but I was just exhausted!"* What? Just because you bought cupcakes for your kid's class instead of making them from scratch does not make you a bad parent!

Neither does missing a soccer match, letting the TV be a babysitter every so often or locking yourself in the bathroom for a few minutes of peace. Most of us are doing the best that we can in a hyper, demanding and overscheduled world.

Living in the Moment

Most of us spend a lot of time pretending that we have it all together while we all wish our lives away. We tell ourselves that it will get easier when the kids are out of diapers, in school, out of school, out of the house, blah blah blah. That's not true! There are wonderful moments through all of these stages which go hand-in-hand with all of the challenges. We miss amazing things when we are not in the moment, focusing on what could be, rather than what is. So of course you've heard that old adage: Be present, because that's the greatest present of all. IT'S TRUE!

Take a Perfection Vacation

So what's the solution? After mucho stress and incredible feelings of guilt, I am finally learning to let go a bit and get a handle on this: Every day we make choices about how to invest our precious time. So... rather than run around like a maniac through my train wreck of a house, I now try to put things into perspective. Sure I could follow behind everyone and pick up everything, but is that really how I want to spend what little free time I have? I could fold laundry or read books to my babes. Should I crank out more e-mails or spend time chatting with my husband?

What I've discovered is that when I let go and take a perfection vacation, I'm letting go of a whole lot of stress and enjoying life a whole lot more!

TWO Fabulous Discoveries:

1. DUST IS NOT MOLD. It's actually a protective covering on my furniture.. And the bonus... the kids have a fresh slate to create their artwork every day.

2. When windows are too clean, birds may fly into them and die.

It's all about perspective!

We Didn't Plan It That Way, But...

The best memories happen when things aren't perfect. My mother-in-law has a great story about the time she was cooking some special pork chops for a big family dinner and made the mistake of hitting the *"CLEAN OVEN"* button. The oven went on lockdown as the cleaning process started with the pork chops still in there. No one could shut it off. Everyone ran around the island yelling and carrying on for the FOUR hours until the oven was finished cleaning – pork chops and all. Not only were the pork chops

amazingly tender
and tasty,
thus adding
some new
instructions to the
recipe card, but everyone
is still talking about that memorable dinner – 20 years later.

As a professional speaker, some of the most memorable times were when crazy things happened... fire alarms, microphone issues, tripping on stage and even wearing my microphone to the bathroom... well, maybe not that one. These *"not perfect"* moments were far more memorable for me and for the audiences than the ones that went as planned! Sometimes *"as planned"* is pretty dull, while the crazy and unexpected provide great "story value" for years to come.

Humorista Hot Tip

Laugh About it NOW!
There are a lot of those, "We're going to laugh about this later" moments that we really should take the time to laugh about right now!

The Good Stuff

6

Taming the House Tornado

Getting organized at work is one thing. Getting organized at home is something else! So often, it's the little things that throw you over the edge. Whether it's deciding what to make for dinner or how to make sense of your closet (all these clothes and nothing to wear!), planning is key.

Sunday Meal Planning

OK folks. Listen, this is not rocket science. It isn't even new news! Sit down. Grab your recipes. Think about what you want the menu to be for the week ahead. Write it on the family calendar so everyone knows what's on deck (hopefully minimizing the tragic, *"I hate tomato soup"* cries of despair).

You may want to try the theme-for-every-night-of- the-week approach that remains constant throughout the month. Monday is Meat (chicken, steak, hamburger, pork), Tuesday is Tacos (or a Mexican dish),

Wednesday is Help Yourself (leftovers and must-go items),
Thursday is casserole, and Friday is Pizza or Pasta night.

So create your list, and
shop in one fell swoop.
This avoids the, *"What the
heck are we going to eat?"*
drama at 4 p.m. every night,
and you're ready to rock-n-
roll for an entire week!

The Missing Ingredient

I am queen of the one missing ingredient. In a remarkable twist of fate,
one night I decided to be fancy and make chicken picatta. Unfortunately,
I didn't have any white wine (what in the world has my life come to?!) but
I did have a bottle of cabernet open. Are you ahead of me? Yes, I used red
wine for my chicken picatta and the chicken turned out pink. The dish
looked awful. Even the capers were embarrassed to be on the same plate.
Instead of pointing out my culinary flaws like I usually do – greeting

everyone with, *"Sorry about the pork chops... I overcooked them,"* or, *"The recipe called for basil... I hope cilantro tastes OK,"* I opted to place the meals in front of my starving family without mentioning the replaced ingredient. The moment I put the flamingo chicken plate in front of my 6-year-old son, he put his hands to his face and started sobbing. *"What's the matter?"* I asked. He could barely spit out his reply, *"I can't eat that. It looks disgusting!"* You know, I've made many culinary errors in my day, but this is the first time anyone has been brought to tears – besides me, that is.

Closets, Pantries and Junk Drawers, OH MY!

Where are my keys? Sunglasses? Remote? Shoes? Misplaced items can make you feel crazy. You aren't crazy (well, maybe a little). You're probably just like the rest of us... running non-stop, multi-tasking and your mind is on a million things at once. Seriously though... have you ever looked for your sunglasses only to find them on your head? Or found yourself yelling at everyone about your misplaced keys, only to discover them in your hand?

Then there are the accumulation situations. What do you have? What do you need? Do you ever throw a package of scotch tape into your grocery cart, only to realize when you get home that you already have seven packages??? Yes, there are two in the junk drawer, three more with the gift wrap, one in the kitchen by the recipe file and still another in your desk with your office supplies. And oh yeah... there's the 12-pack from the wholesale club that was such a great deal, sitting quietly on the shelf in the basement! Does the chaos and over-abundance of stuff in your life make you absolutely insane? Me too!

Here's the plan: if you feel overwhelmed by the lack of organization in your cupboards and drawers, just take one drawer at a time. Now let's get started. Set your timer for 20 minutes each day (yup... just 20 minutes), pick a section of the room you want to address, and go for it! You'll be surprised at what you can accomplish in 20 minutes. For those of you who are list makers, write down the drawers or areas in your house that bug you the most. Not only will you have more focus, you'll feel an extra sense of accomplishment, checking each item off your list.

Get into placement habits. Have some hooks by the garage door where you ALWAYS put your keys. Have a spot by the keys where you ALWAYS put your sunglasses. Store things where you need them. It sounds like common sense, but if you are always going into the garage for something you need quickly, like a flashlight, reconsider its home.

At my house, we seem to go through batteries like water, so I put a drawer in the kitchen dedicated to all things voltage. And get drawer separators so things aren't rolling around in there.

Humorista Hot Tip

What's the Password? Keep a Rolodex or a secret spot with your internet passwords

A Closet Full of Clothes and Nothing to Wear

Is your closet in total chaos? Donate items that no longer fit or that still have tags on them. I once thought that I should buy those sizing circles that they use on racks in boutiques to help me organize my *"fat"* clothes and my *"skinny"* clothes because I often roller coaster in weight. Then I decided to get rid of the *"not gonna go there again"* big sizes as well as the *"one time I had the flu"* tiny clothes. Bring the items you paid-a-lot-of-money-for-even-though-you-never-wore-them-once to the consignment shop or sell them on e-bay. Donate to organizations like Dress for Success that provide business attire for women re-entering the work force.

Purging can be difficult so it helps to get a family member or a good friend with new eyes to give you the thumbs up or thumbs down. My mom still had a drawer full of Krystle Carrington shoulder pads (remember the 80s soap-opera Dynasty?) and dickies (remember those?) that I made her give away. She has yet to call me crying over the loss of her linebacker pads. It feels so good to have a closet cleanse. You probably only wear 10% of your clothes anyway, so clean out the extra for fewer closet meltdown moments. Only keep the things you feel wonderful wearing. Plus, when you can donate the items to a charity or organization in need, the feeling is even better!

Use Humor as a Tool

One of my girlfriends is truly the Imelda Marcos of shoes. When she comes home every day, she faithfully takes them off by the front door. A huge pile develops, driving her husband absolutely crazy. One day she came home expecting the usual shoe argument only to find her shoes on the floor lined up, creating a path into the bedroom and arriving squarely in front of her closet! She laughed hysterically with her husband while picking her shoes up off the shoe trail and putting them away. Message received!

What do you normally complain about and is there a way to use humor to get the point across? Instead of asking people to help, give them specific things you want them to do or choose between. Do you want to fold the laundry or wash the dishes? Do you want to set the table or fill the bird feeder? This way no is not one of the options. Try to make things fun, especially if you have little ones. I've often told my kids we were having a clean room contest. Who can clean their room the quickest? A friend with teenagers takes things that are left around the house and puts them in a locked foot locker. Then the kids get charged to get their items back. She said it works like a charm!

Take a Picture... It'll Last Longer

Is your house overrun with kids' crafts? It's always a dilemma trying to decide what to toss and what should go into the memory box. Then there is the guilt looking into the memory box thinking that it will never truly be organized. Yes, you crafters may have a smug smile right now contemplating your lovely scrapbook collage, but this section is not for you. For the rest of us, try taking pictures of your favorite art work. Then go to one of those web sites that allows you to create a book that contains all of the images. It takes up far less space, and it's really easy to do. Just click and drop the pictures into the book design of your choice. Viola!

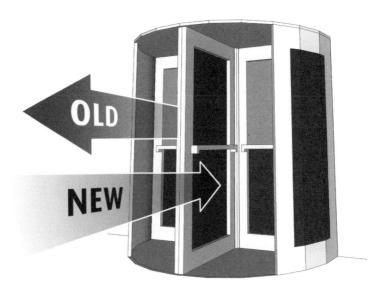

One In, One Out

If you have an influx of kids' toys, make sure you also have an *"outgoing"* system. We have a box for *"boys with no toys"* and when something new arrives, something old must go into the box for a little boy that may not have any toys. Not only does it teach the concept of giving, it helps keep the toy level somewhat tolerable.

And adults... this works for you as well... new sweater in, old sweater out... new shoes in, old shoes out.

Pay For It

Take a look at opportunity cost. Anytime you make a decision to do something, think about what it is you're giving up. Ask yourself, *"Why am I doing what I'm doing right now?"* Often times you find yourself spinning your wheels or working on something that is truly not a priority or doing something that you could hire out. Instead, use the time for something that would give you much joy in return. Living in Texas lends itself to unbearably hot summers. After getting attacked by red ants, getting stung by a scorpion and sweating more than I care to mention, we quickly decided that we could give up something in order to pay for a lawn service. And it was SO worth it! Look for those things in your life that you can hire out. Even if it means taking your lunch to work every day or pulling back on your entertainment budget – you can make smart choices about how to spend your time and dollars!

Forget Paul and Polly Perfect

Spend more time having fun and being with friends and family. We get too worked-up over having everything at home looking like a designer magazine. It just isn't possible.

I always thumb through those magazines and wonder how much fun my two little kids and our 100 lb. doggie could have in those pristine surroundings. I would be a mess thinking about the damage that could be done to those picture perfect rooms. I sigh at the cream carpet in the photo, then look over at Murphy, the chocolate lab who sheds when you look at him. Then I flash back to my Italian grandmother with her plastic-covered couches and plastic runners on her rugs.

Get real and don't worry about being the *"after"* picture. Enjoy life, try to maintain some sense of order and realize that home really stands for **H**opefully **O**rganized, **M**ostly **E**xciting. Live in the moment. And if a home design magazine comes calling, I'll be sure to dust, shove everything into the closet and pray the closet door doesn't come flying open.

The Good Stuff

7

Eliminating
the Chaos

Tame Your Paper

A guru once taught me a wonderful mantra that I've never forgotten. Say this very slowly and pronounce every syllable carefully. *"Fil-ing is NOT meant for stor-age. Fil-ing is meant for re-trie-val!"* Thank you grasshopper – wise words.

While we know in our logical minds that we can retrieve almost anything on the Internet, we still seem obsessed with keeping things *"just in case."* Talk to your accountant. Find out exactly how long to keep financial documents. Do you really need the greeting card that your sister gave you 30 years ago? Maybe compile a scrapbook or *"best of"* and pitch the rest.

Humorista Hot Tip

Feel the urge to paper purge!

The problem is that we keep too many irrelevant things, making it impossible to find the things we really need. Clear out the clutter. Yes, it is overwhelming. Stop telling me how you can't do this because you can. Give it 20 minutes every day and before you know it, your paper nightmares will be under control. And yes, I know there are some important things that you must keep, but stay with me on this one.

Get Vertical

Work on categorizing
your papers. Yes!
Gas receipts go in
a vertical file called
(come on... you can do this)
Gas Receipts. The electric bill
goes in a file called Home Expenses
or Utilities... you get this. Really,
it's just that easy!

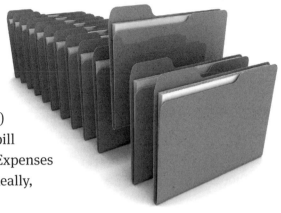

Here's the key to the kingdom:
**Vertical papers get filed and
horizontal ones get piled.**
Now I admit that moving from
horizontal to vertical can be a
challenge. But if you succeed at
getting things into vertical files,
you will have a better chance at
finding what you need and living
amidst far less chaos!

Have a Purge Day

Once a month (some of you may need to do this more often), make time for a quick paper purge. Set timers for a half-hour so this exercise is fast, productive and doesn't get in the way of other things. Convince your office to have a contest to see which department can clear out the most paper. Have everyone clean out desks, cabinets, storage areas, EVERYTHING! Then teams weigh their loot (which will be recycled, of course) and the group with the most paper wins a pizza party or some other fabulous prize!

Everything Needs an Expiration Date

Ever feel like your *"Pending"* file is overwhelming? I have tons of those persnickety documents that I can't toss, don't want to file and have to revisit again and again. What to do? Here's a hot tip: Put an expiration date in the upper right corner of documents you know you'll be able to pitch sooner rather than later. For example, put an expiration date on FedEx and UPS delivery slips 2 weeks after the delivery date. If the person doesn't receive the package, you would have heard something

by that date. So now, instead of doing the mental gymnastics to figure out if you still need to keep the slip, the date allows you to toss it – NOW! How about office memos? Maybe a 3-month expiration date on those puppies and into the shredder they go!?

Three Strike Rule

Many-a-time I've heard that you should touch paper only once, but I live in the real world. As a big fan of the snooze alarm, I like a few chances – at least. With the Three Strike Rule you have two chances to snooze. Here's how it works. When you touch a paper, think, *"Do it, Delegate it or Dump it."* If you aren't ready to do any of those things, then you put a dot in pencil on the lower left corner of the paper. Next time you touch that same paper, go through the three *"Ds"* again. If you STILL aren't ready for action, put another pencil dot in the corner. The third time you touch it, you must DO, DELEGATE OR DUMP. This really works and prevents the insane shuffle where pages mysteriously migrate for very long periods of time from one side of the desk to the other.

Rainbow Files

There are too many manila folders in the workplace and they all blend together into a meaningless fog. Not only is it dull, it provides no information whatsoever! Here's a tip: Use red folders for *"urgent action items,"* yellow for *"on deck"* items and green for the *"when you have time"* projects.

Humorista Hot Tip

Ban manila folders from the workplace!

I have a friend who's taken this one step further. She uses the hot pink ones with white stripes from the Container Store for the urgent items, florals from Target for the on-deck projects and plain brown for the low priority items. Now maybe the extra attention to décor isn't completely necessary but with either scenario, there is some semblance of prioritization and the desk area sure looks prettier!

Rip and Read File

Do you subscribe to magazines because it is SO much cheaper than buying them at the newsstand? Good for you! But here's what happens to me... they come every month and before I know it, I have a 3-year pile of *Oprah* that I'm sure I'll read, eventually. Yeah, right.

What I realized is that the pile was making me feel guilty and draining my energy. So here's what I do to alleviate magazine stress: When I get a magazine or periodical, I thumb through and rip out what looks interesting and relevant. I put those items in a *"Rip and Read"* file and put the mag in a recycle bin. Then I take the file to meetings, doctor appointments and any place where I know I'll be waiting in line.

The Good Stuff

8

Stressbusters

Most of us are looking for that magic pill to relieve our stress – that one big thing that will bring sanity to our lives. Guess what? That one big thing doesn't exist. It's a bunch of little things that you can control! It's so easy to be distracted and overwhelmed in this wild world. And the key is (drum roll here!)... FASTING!

TV, Techno and Facebook Fasting

I know. You hear the word FAST and you're already thinking food. NO NO NO – I don't mean food! I mean those distractions that divide our attention, that add stress and keep us from doing the things we really need to be doing. LET'S FOCUS ON WHAT'S IMPORTANT, PEOPLE! How many times do you run like Pavlov's dog when you hear the *"bing"* on your computer alerting you that a new e-mail has arrived? With my super-powered-INBOX-hearing, I can detect an e-mail arrive from across the house. I promptly become zombie-like, moving toward the computer, *"must check the message — must check the message."* What in the world am I waiting for? Excitement! Anticipation! Who's it from? But usually, it's kind of a bummer. Another J. Crew sale... so what?

Turn off that thing that alerts you! So what would happen if you walked away from your computer and came back in 2 hours? There might be a bunch of e-mails (just like Christmas!) What if? Put a timer by your computer to remind you how long you've been sitting there. Give up late night e-mails. I know you are trying to catch up, but so are a bunch of other overachievers out there. You think you are making some progress at midnight and then people begin to respond. Then you write them back, *"What are you doing up?"* and they write, *"What are you doing up?"* and you write, *"Go to bed,"* and they write, *"No, you go to bed."* ENOUGH! Everyone needs to go to bed! Trust me it will all be there in the morning.

And the TV. How often do you pop on the TV just because? You know what's on... NOT MUCH.

And Facebook... don't get me started! I do love that I can keep up with old cronies and see wonderful pictures from far-flung friends, but every time my Facebook friend fills in that stupid line, *"What's on your mind?"* I get a new post highlighting the minutia in her life. Although I'm compelled to follow her newsfeed instead of CNN, is it really necessary to read every single update? Now, I know that it's important to your BFF to post that she's doing laundry and going to Chipotle for a burrito, but I'm not sure I need to know.

Humorista Hot Tip

Stop Checking & Start Doing!

If you want to lower your stress level immediately, here is the perfect idea. Cut back on all of it – NOW!

News Fasting

Isn't it nice when you're on vacation and you don't carry the weight of the world's problems on your shoulders? We get in the habit of waking up and turning on the news to catch up on all the ills of the night before. *"Your 401(k) is a 101(k). Terror continues, and Britney is on tour."* Yes there is a fire somewhere, a natural disaster somewhere else and bad people are everywhere, doing bad things. Ugh!

How many hours of news do you hear every day? If your day is anything like mine, maybe you turn on the TV to a morning show while you're getting the kids ready or having a cup of coffee. Does this information start your day off right? Not usually. Then we hit the newspaper – more bad news. And to make matters worse, we like to end a hectic day by watching the news one last time before going to sleep. This puts us in a calm, happy and relaxed state. Right.

Yes, we can get news 24/7, but do we really want it? Work on limiting your news fix to ONCE a day. Don't get me wrong... it's important to know what's going on out there, but once pretty much does it for me.

NO News is Good News!

Humorista Hot Tip

Slide it Back!

A friend of mine told me that when he stays at a hotel where they slide the newspaper under his door, he slides it right back out into the hall.

Need Updates? Mom Will Call

If something major is going on, you will hear about it. Really! You may overhear it on the train or in the elevator. Or maybe you'll get the scoop when you drop your kids off at school. In my world, I know I can count on my mom for all of the critical updates. *"Throw out your peanut butter crackers!"* *"Make sure you wash bagged veggies!"* Certainly you have someone in your life who can alert you to life's breaking news stories. No? Send me an e-mail and I'll get you signed-up on mom's *"Things to Worry About"* call list.

The Humorista's Top 10 Ways to Spend All Your Newly-Found Free Time

10 Take a walk

9 Read a book

8 Try a new recipe from one of those 30 recipe books sitting on the shelf that you swore you'd use faithfully

7 Call someone you haven't spoken with in over a year

6 Visit a neighbor

5 Start a jigsaw puzzle (watch and see how everyone joins in!)

4 Take up a new hobby – this could be anything from playing music to photography

3 Volunteer – it's probably your turn!

2 Visit the gym that you've been donating to over the last year

1 Give your family your undivided attention

Humorista Hot Tip

Record the Good Stuff

Listen to music that inspires you to start your day.
DVR your favorite comedy shows and watch that before you go to bed.
Keep a few episodes of "I Love Lucy" or "The Office" handy for veg time.

Cell Phone Etiquette

Sure if you're a new mom and you've left your 3-month-old with a sitter for the first time, everyone will understand that you'll want your cell phone close by. But for the rest of us, why not turn the thing off for a while? You have the voice mail option, right?

"But what if something happens?" Yes, things can, do and will happen, but do you really need to know about them NOW?!

For example, you may get word from your great Aunt Gracie in Gurnee that your dear Uncle Louis has finally passed at the ripe old age of 104. Yes, that's very sad, but guess what? Uncle Louis is already gone. And whether you find out about it this instant, or in an hour after your lunch, makes no difference. Dear Uncle Louis is still gone. And all your luncheon colleagues will like you far better – as you were able to focus on them, rather than being distracted by whatever calls you may or may not get!

Smartphone Affair?

Warning: you may be addicted to your Smartphone. Numerous articles have called the wireless device as addictive as hard drugs. With any addiction, the first step is to admit that you have a problem. If you are oblivious to the world around you when checking messages throughout your day at the expense of productivity and family/friend time – LISTEN UP.

I have a friend who sleeps with her iPhone under her pillow and her husband thinks it's ridiculous. She may end up sleeping with just her iPhone if she isn't careful. Think about how much time is wasted with techno interruptions and how long it takes for you to get back on track, doing things, rather than always checking things. Add up the time – you'll be surprised. Turn off your device at mealtimes, when on an important deadline or when you are not really *"at work."* And for goodness sakes, put an auto message on your devices when you are away on vacation and TAKE A REAL VACATION! You may find the withdrawal effects too much to bear, but it will get better with time. You can do it.

Knife, Fork, Spoon, Smartphone?

Ever notice at restaurants and bars that everyone puts their cell phones on the table. Like it's another eating utensil? What?

C'mon Aretha

Ever hear someone say, *"You make me feel INSERT-EMOTION-HERE?"*

Well wake up! Nobody makes you feel anything. You allow your emotions to take shape. What you say creates your day. If you say, *"I'm having one of those days,"* without a doubt, you will have one of those days! And for the love of Pete, never say, it can't get worse. Oh yeah? Now you've done it – just wait. It can always get worse! If you really want to see how a day can go from nightmarish to unfreakin-believable, check out the story of my traffic ticket /defensive driving school/another ticket/kicked out of class saga at www.ChristineCashen.com/drive.

You Got the Power!

It's NOT about what happens to you. It's what you make of it that really matters.

You, and only you, are in charge of your emotions.

Take the 2-Hour Good Mood Commitment Challenge

Here's what happens. You wake up and you're still exhausted. You go to the refrigerator. You open it up. You take out the orange juice and it's empty. Whatever.

You get in your car and start driving to work. It's obvious that you are the only one who knows how to drive today. Someone cuts you off. Have you ever felt like you're driving during amateur hour?

You get to the office and someone's parked in your parking spot. Your name's not on it, but everybody knows you park there!

Whoa – normally any one of these things would send you into a tailspin. It's a good thing you've taken the 2-Hour Good Mood Commitment Challenge.

You start your day by deciding that regardless of what happens, you are in a good mood, no matter what. You don't have to act like you're in a good mood. You just say it for the first two hours of the day. Come on, you can do it. No whining. Not today. Why? Say it out loud, *"It's a good thing I'm in a good mood."*

So now you have that good mood filter: OJ MIA? No big deal. Maybe today is the day you treat yourself to fresh-squeezed from the deli! Someone took your parking spot? No big deal. You found a better one.

Say Fine and Keep Walking

You have to try this at work. When your coworker asks, *"How are you?"* what does he expect to hear back?

"I'm fine. How are you?"

Well forget about it. He doesn't care. You don't care and it's a waste of human breath. So next time someone asks, try saying, *"I'm in a really great mood!"* Again – just the first two hours of the day. And keep walking.

It's fun to watch the reactions. But be prepared to be followed down the hall. Really! People become curious and chase you down, *"You're in a great mood? What makes you so happy? Hey! Are you leaving?!"*

Nothing is better than when someone has something positive to say. I remember passing a custodian in the hallway at work and greeting him with the usual, *"How are you?"* routine and he responded, *"If I were any better, I'd be twins!"* It stopped me in my tracks. What? I got a huge smile on my face and was still smiling when I went into my meeting, and I had a fun story to tell. The story lightened up the meeting. It had a trickle down effect! So, look out. Attitudes are contagious. What if the custodian had replied with a list of complaints? I would have walked into my meeting with a totally different vibe, thus changing the entire mood of the meeting.

Don't be a buzzkill. We all have issues. *"You didn't sleep at all last night? Well, I haven't slept in over 4 years, so lucky for you!"* As tempting as it can be to get involved in the *"My story is worse than your story"* routine, it's a huge downer and a total waste of time. Tell these people to save the drama for their mamas! Create some good karma and take the first step toward a good mood commitment. You will find that when the two hours are up, you really do feel better. Sure it's a *"Fake it 'til you make it"* strategy but amazingly, it really works! Then sit back and watch the good vibes spread.

Whine for Wine

Get a jar. Cut out a piece of paper and write in big fat letters, WHINE JAR. Tape it on the jar and place it in the most visible spot on your desk. Tell everyone who comes within a mile of your desk that the new law is: Every time you complain, you must put a dollar in the Whine Jar. At the end of the month, use the cashola for some real wine or another fun treat. It will definitely reduce negative chatter.

Sit on the Stairs Until You're Happy!

You know that you have the power to change your attitude, right? Absolutely. You may not always want to change it, but that's your choice. So I decided that if I want to affect attitudes, I should first start locally – with myself, my family and then maybe take on the world.

So right now I'm still in family mode. At the Cashen house, when the kids become whiney, we take the *"Sit on the stairs until you're happy"* approach. It's a bit of a crack-up when my little girl is sent to the stairs after griping, complaining and fussing about not getting a cookie, and she walks by me rubbing her eyes while growling, *"I'm a happy girrrllll!"*
I have to remind her to tell her face, because she doesn't look very happy. So she sits on the stairs for a few more minutes. I inevitably peek around the corner and ask, *"Are you happy yet?"* and she mopes, *"Not yet."* Then I go about my business and she pops around the corner with a huge smile, *"I'M HAPPY NOW!"* and runs over to give me a hug. I usually tell her that I missed her while she was on the stairs, and I'm glad to have my happy girl back again.

Wouldn't it be great to use this sit on the stairs method with your co-workers or employees? *"Hey you, go sit on the stairs until you're happy!"* The gloomy employee enters the stairwell to find there are 12 other people sitting there too. Someone scoots over so she can sit down. She asks the person next to her, *"So how long have you been here?"* He replies, *"Three years."*

Smile File

Do you ever need a quick positive mental shake-up? Here is a fast and easy stress buster. It doesn't take a lot of time, but yields great dividends. You need to have a Smile File. This is a folder where you keep positive letters from clients, friends and family members. You keep those, right? You can also include funny cards, cartoons and news stories. Whenever you run into that annoying person – whether it's a boss, client or just Joe-Jerk-on-the-street – pull out the file for a mini-mental vacation.

Fabio's Roller Coaster Debacle

Truth-be-told: some of the news stories I've clipped for my Smile File are things that I think are funny, but may actually be on the fringe of good taste and political correctness. A few years ago, there was an article about Fabio, the male model. He was at Busch Gardens for the grand opening of a new roller coaster. Strategically seated in the front row with his white shirt unbuttoned to the middle of his chest, Fabio was surrounded by young women wearing angelic white outfits. Well, mid-ride a bird flew right into Fabio's face. Okay, it wasn't just a bird... it was a goose! What a terrible accident, right? OMG, Fabio's nose was broken and the bird was killed – but for some reason I laughed until I leaked. I know it's wrong, but that's what happened. In fact, the day after the story ran, I was on a plane and the guy next to me opened up his *USA Today* and there's a picture of Fabio, in his open shirt, surrounded by *"angels"* bloodied.

The caption read, *"Fabio was goosed in the honker."* It sent me into an uncontrollable laughing fit that I could not contain! Have you ever tried to hold back and you just get more giggles? Painful!

At a recent event I told this story and a woman shouted out, *"He had killer looks!"* and I lost it all over again. It's the gift that keeps on giving. Sorry, Fabio.

Take a FUN RUN

This is for all of you after-hours workers, sitting at your desks, having a pity party saying, *"No one appreciates all I do here. This is crazy, I should go home. I need a life."* Or, if you're sitting at home with a million things to do, but you decide to sit down for just a second... this tip is for you!

When you need a burst of energy to kick you into gear, go on a FUN RUN. It takes only 30 seconds, so no excuses about not having enough time. Here you go... remain seated and begin running in place. First, start with your legs and then add your arms. If you really want to get the blood flowing, raise your arms over your head. 30 seconds is longer than you think, but don't give up. Keep going and don't forget to do a slow, gradual cool down.

Feel your heart beating? The blood will flow down to your legs and back up to your brain, helping you to think more clearly. This quick energizer is just what you need when you're stuck both mentally and physically.

That's right. Now get busy and finish up what's keeping you stuck. Get off the couch! Go home and get a life! You deserve it!

WARNING: If you do this at work while other people are around, they may come take work away from you.

ANOTHER WARNING: Be careful if you have wheels on your chair. You may end up on a modified secret mission!

ONE MORE WARNING: At home, your family will think you have lost your marbles, but that's okay.

Wish I Was STILL There

A girlfriend of mine sends herself postcards every time she goes on vacation. Really! She usually sends them to her office. They always say the same thing, *"Wish You Were Here!"* and she means it! Whenever things get stressful, she pulls out her file, thumbs through her postcards and mentally travels right back to that beach, gorgeous vista or fantastic getaway. When she closes the file, she feels refreshed and at peace.

The Humorista's Top 10 Must Haves for Your Smile File

10 Wacky newspaper articles

9 Cartoons that crack you up

8 Happy fortune cookie messages

7 Pet pix that didn't make it to your desk

6 Great letters from clients, friends and family

5 That greeting card you just couldn't throw away

4 An e-mail that's been forwarded 300x that really is funny

3 Vacation postcards

2 Goofy pictures of yourself – bonus points if you are under 5-years-old and have food on your face, or you're naked in the bath tub!

1 Heck it's your file... whatever you want!

Smile Trial

On my recent trip to NYC with my fellow Dallas book club crew, we found ourselves discussing attitudes of New Yorkers. For me, the NY attitude is merely a myth, but others disagreed.

To prove my point, I challenged my group to take the Smile Trial. Here's how it works: whenever you approach someone, put a big, warm smile on your face as if you were greeting an old friend, and see what transpires.

Everyone was a bit skeptical, but once they saw how it played out, everyone was in on the plan. We'd walk by buildings and wave at doormen inside. We greeted subway toll booth operators with smiles, and struck up conversations with strangers. It was so much fun to crack the ice on the faces of so many unsuspecting and confused people. Everyone responded really well except for one guy in the subway. We thought he was ignoring us, but then to our surprise, he took off his hat and we saw that he was wearing earphones. *"Are you talking to me?"* he asked. By the end of the ride, we'd made a new friend.

You get what you expect in most situations. Look for people to be open, kind and friendly but FIRST, try exhibiting those characteristics yourself! By the end of the NYC book club weekend, I think I'd successfully busted-up the New York attitude myth with my Dallas book club chums, and we were counting the days until our next trip back.

Don't Trap the Gas!

Never, ever hold in your laughter. The suppressed air gets trapped. It then works its way through your body, making you bloated and puffy. To make matters worse, you never know where it may get trapped and at what embarrassing moment it will come out. For all of our sakes, laugh loud and often!

Afterburner

Whew, so there you have it. Did you have a good time and learn something new? I appreciate your taking me home with you. Keep **The Good Stuff** handy when you need a quick pick-me-up or great idea. Don't be stingy – share the Humorista Hot Tips... well, maybe not the "Secret Mission" or you may get busted. Come back and visit often... I'll miss you. Now, go get the "good stuff" out of life every day – you deserve it!

Acknowledgements

Hugs to mom, dad and my brother for all the great support, laughter and providing a life full of material.

Special thanks to Saint Gregg, my hubby. You are the yang to my yin and the perfect partner for all my adventures. Much love to my kids for dragging me out of my office to play. It is a privilege to be your mom.

To all the Book Fairies who helped me birth this project: Mere words cannot convey enough thanks for my editor, Debbie Johnson. You were the driving force behind all aspects of this book. Not only are you smart and funny, you are a great friend and a really cool chick. The illustrations from one of the most talented women I know, Tami Evans, are over the top fantastic – and so is she. Kudos to Alan Jazak and his Formation Studio crew for putting their *designs* on me. Also to Karen Rawlins, proofreader extraordinaire. And to Karla Sheppard – you have great eyes.

Ed Primeau (Primeau Productions), you have been there from the beginning, and I appreciate your friendship more than you know.

Even if my book bud Bobbe White got her TWO books out before I typed my first word, I am forever grateful for the push needed to get this book off of my mind and into print.

I have had many great teachers, supporters and friends along the way (you know who you are dahlings), but let me give an extra shout out to: Barbara Braunstein, Carole and Howard Greisdorf, Hapi Kendall and my CMU crew Doc Allen, Betty Wagner and Dan Eversole. Cheers to my Dallas book club babes, Twin Coves neighbors, NSA-NT and our family angel, Stacie Powdermaker.

Hugs to a few folks who have provided great ideas and unbridled enthusiasm: the *GiveaGeta* guy, Jim Cantoni; *Watchdog Nation* author, Dave Lieber; Earth People's Anna Clark; Lisa Rowe from *The Perfect Image* and Tim Durkin.

Special thanks to those people who spread joy by going through life with a sense of humor – that would be you Steve at the Flower Mound Post Office. Also, those who BOOGIE every day, like Mohamed Adatia and his beautiful family, former owners of the Nestle Tollhouse Café in Highland Village – you rock!

I can't forget the amazing audiences and event planners who have allowed me to share my good stuff on stage for over 15 years. And thanks to you Cool Reader for picking up **The Good Stuff!** Your questions, letters and book-group invitations (I can attend via Skype) are always welcome. Drop me a line at Christine@ChristineCashen.com and tell me your "good stuff"!

—Christine

About the Author

Christine Cashen delivers a fast-paced, hilarious program with useful content that makes her a sought after speaker worldwide. For more than 15 years, she has jazzed an amazing variety of audiences throughout the United States, Canada, South Africa and Australia. Christine is an authority on sparking innovative ideas to handle conflict, reduce stress and energize employees.

Before hitting the speaking scene, Christine was a university admissions officer, corporate trainer and broadcaster. Hey – she even votes. She holds a Bachelors Degree in Communication and a Masters Degree in Adult Education. Christine is a member of the National Speakers Association and is a Certified Speaking Professional (CSP), an earned designation held by fewer than 10% of the speakers on the planet.

What makes Christine unique is the *"real"* factor. She combines a down-to-earth attitude with a colorful artistic streak. Comments from audience members such as *"I feel like I've known her forever," "We must take her back to our workplace,"* and *"It felt as if Christine was speaking directly to me,"* are a testament to her effectiveness and style.

Christine has been featured as a creativity expert in *HOW Designs at Work* magazine and is a co-author of the book *Mission Possible, Volume Eight.* She has also developed the A Dynamic Speaker series of learning resources: *Get What You Want With What You've Got* DVD, *The Fun Factor* DVD, *Why Can't Everybody Just Get Along* CD and *Got Humor* Video. Christine resides in Dallas with her husband, their two children and Murphy, the chocolate lab.

For more information on bulk educational product purchases or to hire Christine for your next event, call 800.706.0152.